ICK!

Grossest Science Ever

ISBN: 978-1-338-54706-1

10 9 8 7 6 5 4 3 2 1   19 20 21 22 23

Printed in Guangzhou, China 173
First printing, 2019

Book produced by Scout Books & Media Inc
Written by Susan Knopf
Designed by Dirk Kaufman
Photo research by Brittany Schachner
Copyedited and fact-checked by Beth Adelman

CONTENTS

TERROR IN THE SKIES
A single locust can eat its weight in food every day. Locust swarms are problems in parts of North Africa, the Middle East, and Asia.

Wild Webs Thousands of spiderwebs covered the town of Aitoliko, Greece, in September 2018. Warm, humid weather led to a thriving mosquito population that provided food for the spiders.

THE BIG ICK

What makes something seem icky? It may be because of how it smells. Or maybe it tastes yucky. And sometimes just thinking about something is a total gross-out. There are good reasons why we have these reactions, and *ICK! Grossest Science Ever* will give you the inside scoop.

Some of the biggest icks are swarms and infestations. What's the difference? A swarm is a large number of insects that gather or move together. Mayflies emerge from rivers and lakes in massive swarms that can even be detected by weather radar. Locust and grasshopper swarms devour plants and crops. Other animals can exhibit swarm-like behavior, such as a huge flock of birds traveling together or a colony of bees on the move.

An infestation is a large number of pests that cause problems or diseases in a place or on a host. Termites and mice can infest a house. Lice can infest kids in a classroom. And an Asian longhorn beetle infestation can damage or destroy certain types of trees in a backyard, town, park, or city.

Fortunately, these big icks aren't common in our daily lives. But there are many yucky, gross, and downright disgusting things going on around us all the time. Learn how athletes blow snot rockets when they don't have tissues handy, what eyelash mites are and if they're really pooping on your face at night, and what the yuckiest stuff is lurking in the bathroom.

Turn the page and prepare to say, "Ick!"

BUG-LICIOUS

VALUE MEALS

1 Grasshopper Burger
with Mealworms

Grasshopper Nutrition Facts
Serving Size: 3.5 ounces (99 grams)

Amount per Serving	
Protein	20.6 grams
Fat	6.1 grams
Carbohydrates	3.9 grams

Source: Time.com

2 Grasshopper
Tortilla

OH NO HE DIDN'T!

Competitors ate fried insects including locusts, bamboo worms, dragonfly larvae, and silkworm chrysalises during a competition in Lijiang, China. A man from Chongqing won a gold bar after eating 2.7 pounds (1.2 kilograms) of insects in five minutes!

DESSERTS

5 Mealworm Brownies

6 Cricket Macarons

7 Grasshopper Tarts

8 Cricket Muffins

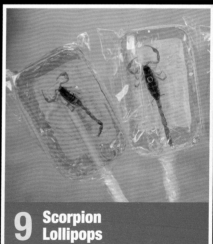

9 Scorpion Lollipops

AH-CHOO!

A sneeze is a wet, slimy spray of mucus. It's also a mini full-body workout that involves the throat, neck, chest, abdomen, and diaphragm. Sneezing is gross, but also good. It clears out things that irritate your nose and helps keep you healthy. So when you feel a sneeze coming, let it fly. But don't use your hands to cover your nose—they'll get too germy. Sneeze into your elbow.

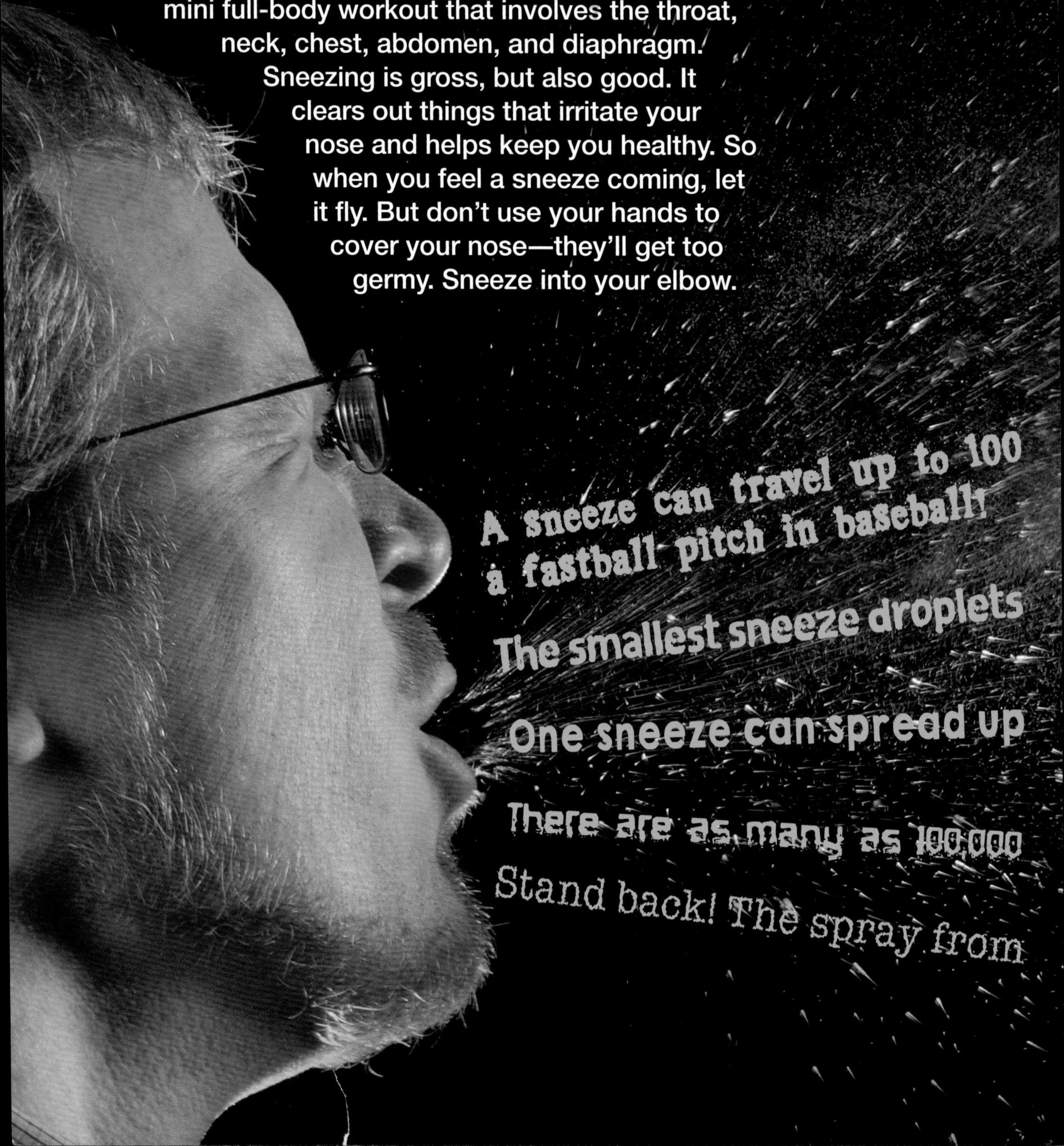

A sneeze can travel up to 100 a fastball pitch in baseball!

The smallest sneeze droplets

One sneeze can spread up

There are as many as 100,000

Stand back! The spray from

BEST SNEEZER

Marine iguanas! They sneeze to get rid of excess salts that accumulate when they digest food.

miles (about 161 kilometers) per hour. That's as fast as

can linger in the air for several minutes in a "puff cloud."

to 100,000 germs (more if you have a cold or flu).

droplets of different sizes in a single sneeze.

a sneeze can travel up to 26 feet (8 meters).

BIG 10! MY BODY

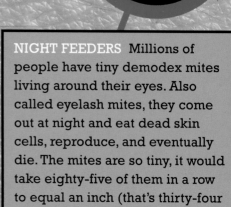

SPLISH SPLASH Our hands pick up germs from everything we touch. Most of the germs that make us sick are spread by the hands. Cold and flu viruses live on the hands for up to an hour.

NIGHT FEEDERS Millions of people have tiny demodex mites living around their eyes. Also called eyelash mites, they come out at night and eat dead skin cells, reproduce, and eventually die. The mites are so tiny, it would take eighty-five of them in a row to equal an inch (that's thirty-four mites to equal a centimeter).

JAM-TASTIC All kinds of junk goes into toe jam, the stuff that collects between the toes: dead skin cells, sock lint, natural body oils, fungus, and bacteria.

THE OUTER LAYER We shed nearly one million skin cells a day. But never fear, our skin is always making new cells, and the cells in the outer layer—the epidermis—are replaced every month. Where do all those dead skin cells go? Tiny dust mites eat them. When dead skin cells clog the pores, pimples can form.

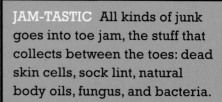

DOES WHAT?

WAX JOB How do you avoid getting dust and other gunk in your ears? Earwax does the job. It keeps things away from the sensitive inner ear. It also prevents dry, itchy ears.

IT SNOT JUST YOU We produce a fresh batch of mucus every twenty minutes—more than a quart a day! It comes from the nose, throat, and lungs. Where does it go? Into the stomach. Ew!

BUUUURP Eating or drinking too quickly, chewing gum, or drinking soda can cause extra air to build up inside the body. Burping lets it all out.

EVERYONE DOES IT . . . A LOT Gas forms as part of the digestion process. Our bodies release it fifteen or more times a day—even at night while sleeping. The gas we pass is mostly odor-free.

SWEAT SPOT Sweat is good—it helps keep our bodies cool. Believe it or not, sweat itself doesn't smell. A big part of our sweat is salt and water. But the sweat glands in the armpits (and groin) produce an oily sweat that attracts bacteria. When the bacteria break down the sweat, body odor forms.

LET'S EAT! Why does your stomach sometimes let everyone know you're hungry? The tummy rumbles when stomach juices churn and muscles contract, getting ready for food.

Lice Aren't Nice!

Is something bugging you? These bloodsucking creepy-crawlies look for animal hosts to feast on—including humans. Here's a collection of some of the smallest troublemakers.

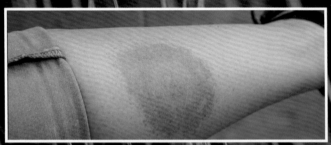

TICKS Ticks can transmit diseases, such as Lyme and Rocky Mountain spotted fever, from one person to another or from an animal to a person. They anchor their teeth and mouthparts into the skin as they burrow in and suck out blood.

Head lice eggs

LICE Lice travel by crawling from person to person through contact or on shared combs, towels, and even hats. They live on scalps near hair roots, where they bite and drink blood. Lice bites make the scalp super itchy.

FLEAS These tiny acrobats are smaller than a grain of rice and can jump more than 7 inches (18 centimeters) in the air as they travel from one host to another. The family pet is a typical target. Fleas can cause allergic reactions and transmit diseases, including bubonic plague.

CHIGGERS These little red mites don't bite—they drill into the skin with their mouthparts, release a special salivary fluid that breaks down the flesh around the hole, then slurp up the goo. After a couple of days, they fall off and wait for another host to wander by.

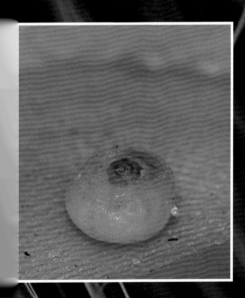

CHIGOE FLEAS Chigoe fleas burrow under the skin and latch on. But they're not interested in blood—they feed on the skin itself.

BEDBUGS Bedbugs hide out in mattresses and feast on sleeping people. They don't have wings and can't jump, but they can travel about 50 feet (15 meters) in a night looking for a warm body to feed on. Their bites are often itchy and painful.

HAIRY AND HORRIBLE

Spiders aren't interested in people, and for most people the feeling is mutual. But there are reasons some find these eight-legged creatures absolutely disgusting.

Unpredictable Movements with no obvious pattern are alarming.

Dark Color Most people think brightly colored ladybugs are beautiful, but find a hairy arachnid icky!

Long Legs People prefer rounded or curved shapes. Angular legs are scary!

TRUE OR FALSE?

If it has eight legs, it's a spider.

False! All arachnids, a group that includes ticks and scorpions, have four pairs of legs.

The Darwin's bark spider has the toughest silk of any spider. Its web is twice as strong as other spiderwebs, and ten times stronger than a bulletproof vest.

STRONGEST WEB

WARNING
DOUBLE TROUBLE

Some things are both gross and scary. The markings on these venomous arachnids say STAY AWAY!

Black Widow Spider
Latrodectus mactans
👁 Red hourglass marking

Brown Widow Spider
Latrodectus geometricus
👁 Dark bands on legs

Red-Legged Widow Spider
Latrodectus bishopi
👁 Reddish-orange head, thorax, and legs

Brown Recluse Spider
Loxosceles reclusa
👁 Violin marking on its back

Sydney Funnel-Web Spider
Atrax robustus
👁 Shiny head and thorax

PESTS Insects are attracted to food, and some get into the packaging before it reaches your kitchen. Red flour beetles can be found in flour, grains, and cereals.

SALT AND PEPPER SHAKERS Scientists at the University of Virginia studying cold and flu viruses found germs on 100 percent of salt and pepper shakers in homes where someone was sick.

SPONGE Studies show that kitchen sponges contain anywhere from millions to billions of bacteria per square inch (about 6.5 square centimeters). Experts recommend replacing sponges frequently.

ANT Ants are omnivores, which means they eat both plants and meat. But many are especially attracted to something sweet, like a sugar jar.

REFRIGERATOR When food gets warm, bacteria can grow. That's why refrigerators need to be kept at or below 40° Fahrenheit (4.4° Celsius).

MESSES

MEAT Raw or undercooked meat can have bacteria that make people sick, with long names such as campylobacter, listeria, and salmonella (shown here).

MOLD Molds are fungi (like mushrooms), and there are about 100,000 different kinds! Moldy food like bread, yogurt, and jam can make people sick. But while you shouldn't eat it, moldy bread played a role in the discovery of antibacterial medicines.

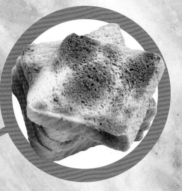

DISHWASHER DOOR Studies have shown that certain fungi, known as yeasts, thrive on dishwasher doors. Causes include the dishwasher's high heat and moisture.

WORM Insect larvae can bore their way into fruit while it's on the tree, then find their way into your kitchen. Look for telltale holes in the skin.

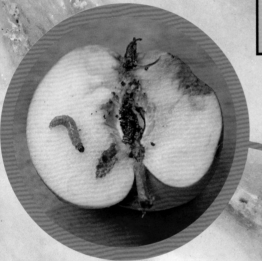

COCKROACH These insects can live for a month without food, but when they find it they will eat almost anything. On a farm in China, 300 million cockroaches eat food waste from restaurants—a case of natural recycling!

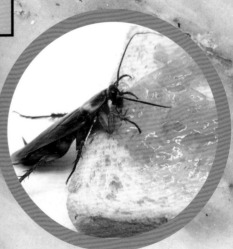

SPIT TAKES

Just like people, animals spit for different reasons. Sometimes they need to clear things out of their mouths, sometimes they spit to say "Back off!", and sometimes they spit to stun or kill prey.

CUTIE PATOOEY An alpaca may look cute, but it has a not-so-cute way of warning off others. It first raises its head and flattens its ears. This is called a standoff position. If that doesn't do the trick, it will shoot out a puff of air. And finally, it spits out a gooey green liquid from its stomach that can travel up to 10 feet (about 3 meters).

SPRAY IT AWAY As walruses swim along the ocean floor, they shoot powerful jets of water to clear away sand and uncover clams underneath. This helps them find the more than 4,000 clams adult walruses can eat in a single feeding.

DEAD AIM A Mozambique spitting cobra can stop a predator in its tracks with venom-laced spit. The snake aims for the eyes and shoots its spit up to 5 feet (about 1.5 meters), blinding the other animal. Researchers report a remarkable 90 percent accuracy in the snake's aim! Then the cobra moves in and injects venom into the flesh with its fangs.

Hosed The archerfish can judge distance from beneath the water and aim with incredible accuracy. It lurks below the water's surface looking for an insect or spider nearby. When it spots one, *whoosh*! A powerful jet of water hits the prey in the eye and kills it. The tasty treat drops into the water for the waiting archerfish.

BIG 10! STINK-EROO

THE NOSE KNOWS Some foods smell so bad, it's hard to imagine anyone would eat it. While there are up to 8,000 taste buds on your tongue and epiglottis (the skin flap at the back of your throat that covers the windpipe), your nose knows something about taste too. It works together with the taste buds to communicate flavor.

CHEESE IT Limburger cheese is loved for its taste but not its smell. As part of the ripening process, it's smeared with the same bacteria that makes feet stink, Brevibacterium linens.

THE BIG STINK Sulfur is in a lot of foods that we eat without knowing it. But it gets smelly when cooking vegetables like broccoli, collard greens, and brussels sprouts. The longer they're cooked, the stinkier they get.

PUNGENT PUNCH Vinegar is used in foods like salad dressing and barbecue sauce, but on its own it packs a pungent smell. Its main ingredient is a chemical compound called acetic acid. This makes it a good cleaner and deodorizer too!

GETTING THE BLUES Blue-veined cheese is smelly and has a strong taste that comes from organisms such as yeast and mold. Yes, that blue vein grows inside the cheese. This may sound icky at first, but lots of people like it.

BANNED! Durian fruit is so smelly it is banned on public transportation, hotels, and airports in areas of Southeast Asia where it is plentiful. More than fifty chemicals work together to make it stink. But its custard-like flesh is full of vitamins and minerals.

KEEP THE LID ON Kimchi is a Korean dish made from cabbage and spices that are left to ferment over weeks or months. It may smell like dirty socks, so keeping it outside in a covered pot is the traditional way to make and store it.

OOEY AND GOOEY A healthy breakfast in Japan may well include nattō. This slimy, smelly food made from fermented soybeans is high in protein, vitamins, and minerals.

SWEDISH FISH Surströmming is a popular dish in Sweden with a smell that lingers. Herring and salt are combined, and the fish ferments for six months to a year—first in a barrel, then in cans.

IN NAME ONLY A traditional Chinese food, century eggs aren't really 100 years old. But they are preserved for several weeks or months, which gives them a strong odor, dark color, and gelatinous texture.

LOOK OUT ABOVE ...AND BELOW!

NOT COOL COOL Black vultures, turkey vultures, and marabou storks have a unique and disgusting way of cooling off. They let their poop dry on their legs. This helps lower their body temperature.

BATHROOM BEHAVIOR A puffin builds a soft, feather-lined nest at the back of its burrow, and a separate toilet area near the front. This helps it keep clean—dirty feathers could damage this seabird's built-in waterproofing.

Male hippos swing their tails like propellers to spread their poop around. They do this to mark their territory and to impress female hippos.

SPLATTER ZONE

MOST ACTIVE POOPER

PROJECTILE POO
How does an osprey keep things tidy? It backs up to the edge of the nest or roost and shoots out projectile poop.

The Scoop On Bird Poop What we think of as bird poop is actually a mixture of solid and liquid waste—they poop and pee at the same time.

TRUE OR FALSE?

You can see penguin poop from space.

True! Adélie penguins eat lots of pink-colored krill (small crustaceans). This makes their poop pink. An image from space helped scientists locate a new colony of more than 1.5 million Adélie penguins. The tip-off? You guessed it, their pink poop!

I LOVE MY PET, BUT ...

THAT'S HAIRY! When a cat bathes itself, hook-like barbs on the tongue trap loose hairs and some are swallowed. Most pass through the digestive system and into the litter box, but those that stay in the stomach are eventually vomited up as a hairball. Hairballs are tube-shaped so they can pass through the esophagus.

THERE'S A RAT IN MY FREEZER! Some pet snakes eat mice and rats. Since live prey can harm a snake in an enclosure, feeding frozen prey can be a safe alternative.

A TROPHY—FOR ME? Cats born in the wild learn to hunt when their mothers bring home dead or injured prey. If you have an outdoor cat, it may bring you a trophy, such as a dead mouse. It may seem gross, but it's simply exhibiting behavior learned from Mom.

Cool Drool Dog drool can be a sign of a medical problem, but in some breeds it's natural. The shape and skin flaps of an English Mastiff's mouth cause a river of drool. Watch out—a good head toss can send the slippery saliva flying!

WRETCHED WHEN WET Dogs are hosts to lots of microorganisms—yeasts and bacteria—that produce a waste-like compound. When dogs get wet, the water mixes with this compound. As it evaporates, it releases that unmistakable wet-dog odor.

BIG 10! THE DIRT

SWEAT IT OUT People lose about a quart of sweat per hour of exercise. Studies show that long-distance runners sweat faster and more per sweat gland, and even ice hockey players on cold rinks sweat a lot due to the fast-paced play and heavy equipment.

DIRTY DUGOUTS The floor of a professional baseball dugout is littered with junk: discarded cups, sunflower seed shells, chewing gum, and even spit. Yuck!

HOT AND STICKY Yoga is strengthening and rejuvenating. One style is also sweaty and smelly. Hot yoga is done in a studio where the temperature tops 105° Fahrenheit (about 40° Celsius).

IN THE SWIM Some competitive swimmers admit to peeing in the water. One in five adults admit to peeing in a pool too. Experts say: Don't do it! It's not only gross, it can make people sick.

SNOT ROCKETS When a long-distance runner has a runny nose and no tissue, a "snot rocket" is the answer. The athlete plugs one nostril with a finger and blows snot out the other, so it travels a safe distance away.

ON SPORTS

IN THE RING A study of US high schools showed that more than 70 percent of skin infections occurred in wrestling. It involves skin contact with others, the mat, and equipment—all potential sources of infection.

PUKE BUCKET When physical exertion, extreme heat, heavy equipment, or dehydration make an athlete feel sick, it's time to tell the coach, take a break, and get help. If an athlete vomits during a game, that's not good for anyone!

DON'T DROP IT A mouth guard protects an athlete's teeth, lips, and tongue. But if it drops in the dirt, studies show it encounters a lot of yucky stuff, including animal feces.

KEEPING IT CLEAN After a professional football game, equipment staff collect sweaty shoulder pads and uniforms that are stained with grass, grime, sweat, and sometimes blood.

LUCKY JERSEY An athlete may think a jersey or other item is lucky and refuse to wash it, wearing it game after game. It's a germy risk, but it may be a form of positive thinking.

SKUNK CABBAGE

Releases an odor that smells like a skunk when it blooms and when a leaf or petal is crushed or bruised

Odor attracts pollinators and keeps away animals that might crush it underfoot

STINKING CORPSE LILY

Smells like rotting meat

Parasitic plant that latches onto vines and then grows inside of them

Blossom can weigh up to 24 pounds (about 11 kilograms)

FLOWER FAILS

▲ Carrion flowers stink to attract insects that spread their pollen.

SUNDEW

Leaves have sticky hairs that attract and trap insects for food

Can kill a trapped insect in about fifteen minutes

PITCHER PLANT

Slippery edges cause an insect to fall into the glue-like fluid in the pitcher

Tentacles wrap around the insect, gripping more tightly as the insect struggles and is eventually eaten

CORPSE FLOWER

Doesn't release its foul odor until it blooms, attracting dung and carrion beetles as pollinators

According to the Guinness Book of World Records, the tallest bloom was a corpse flower that measured 10 feet 2.25 inches (3.1 meters) tall

▼ Tourist traps are sticky plants that trap and usually eat insects.

STICKY COLUMBINE

Attracts insects like flypaper as self-defense, rather than for food

Insect predators like spiders arrive to eat the insects, leaving the plant alone

OH NO THEY DIDN'T!

When a corpse flower blooms at a botanical garden, thousands of people come to smell it . . .

. . . even though it's a smelly adventure.

GROSS GARBAGE

FAST FACTS
GARBAGE IN THE US

✔ Americans produce more than 500 billion pounds (about 227 billion kilograms) of garbage a year (*epa.gov*).

✔ A family of four generates 120 pounds (about 54 kilograms) of garbage a week.

✔ There are 2,000 active landfills.

✔ The largest landfill, in Las Vegas, Nevada, receives 14 million pounds (about 6.4 million kilograms) of garbage a day.

✔ About 300 million pounds (about 136 kilograms) of food is thrown away or composted every year.

✔ Landfills attract animals looking for food—from insects and birds to small and large mammals.

RACCOON

CROW

RAT

BEAR

TRUE OR FALSE?

There are three Rs in garbage.

False . . . but sort of true. To get a handle on garbage, Reduce, Reuse, and Recycle.

BLOWFLIES

SEAGULL

COYOTE

VOLE

PAY DIRT The flu virus can live on a dollar bill for up to seventeen days. US paper money is made from cotton and linen, making it a soft place for microbes to land.

KEYED UP Laptops and desktop computers don't just look dirty from finger smudges and food crumbs. They also pick up germs from hands. And the vents attract dust.

AT THE MARKET Shopping carts come in contact with raw meat, diapers on babies sitting in them, and germs from customers who used them before you.

CAN YOU HEAR ME NOW? Your phone has ten times as many germs as a public toilet! And if you use it in the bathroom, it can pick up even more germs there—so don't!

TOUCH PAD TROUBLES If cash is germy, are ATMs better? A study in New York City found evidence of human skin, microbes from bathrooms, and food on ATMs.

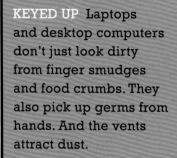

UCH THAT!

CHILLAXING Remote controls are hard to clean. And in homes and hotel rooms, they fall on the floor, are used while eating, and are handled by lots of different people.

BRUSH IT OFF If toothbrushes are left out in the open within a few feet of the toilet, they pick up airborne germs every time it's flushed.

HEADS UP A shower head sends out jets of hot water, which makes it seem like a hard place for things to grow. But some fungi and bacteria thrive in the dark and damp.

FETCH When Fido or Fluffy play with toys, they roll them around in the dust and dirt. A squeaky toy gets a lot of slobber too. And wet toys are breeding grounds for other germs to grow.

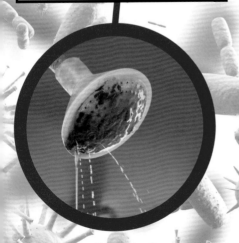

ON/OFF It's no surprise that light switches get dirty. Everyone who touches them deposits germs from their hands. Light switches are among the dirtiest things found in hotel rooms.

SPRAY YOUR TROUBLES AWAY

Skunks may be the most familiar animals that spread their scent around with a foul-smelling spray. But many animals spray when threatened, to mark their territory, or to attract a mate.

LITTLE STINK BOMBS Bombardier beetles release stink bombs that can travel up to 22 miles per hour (about 35 kilometers per hour). The spray is hot—about 212° Fahrenheit (100° Celsius)—and shoots out from the backside. They can release several stink bombs in a row.

TAIL WINDS Female woodhoopoes have an unusual way of protecting their nests. They produce foul-smelling brown oil that can be sprayed from a special gland under the tail.

Striped polecats have scent glands on their backsides that can squirt a large amount of super stinky spray. The smell lingers on the polecat after it sprays, further deterring attackers.

All Charged Up It takes skunks more than a week to recharge their supply of spray, so they first try to ward off potential attackers by raising and shaking their tails, stamping their feet, and displaying their backsides. As a last resort, they release a spray that can be smelled a mile away.

STINKING UP THE PLACE
Stinkbugs head indoors when cooler weather arrives in the fall. When threatened or killed, stinkbugs release a foul odor that can smell rancid, like rotten eggs, or like ammonia.

BIG 10! SCHOOL

BUBBLING BACTERIA Water fountains are the most used but least disinfected spots in schools. Never put your mouth directly on the spigot—that's where most of the bacteria lurk.

FAUCET TROUBLES When you turn on water to wash your hands, you're touching germs from people who've touched the faucet handles over the previous forty-eight hours. That's fine before you wash up—after, use a paper towel to turn the water off.

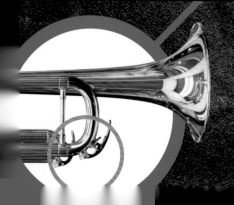

DIRTY CARRY Schools work hard to keep things clean and safe, but cafeteria lunch trays can be dirty places. One study found more than 33,000 bacteria per square inch (about 6.5 square centimeters)—ten times more than on a toilet seat.

WATER MUSIC Trumpets and other brass instruments have a problem with condensation from the player's breath. It needs to be drained during play by opening a water key. It's also called a spit valve, which sounds grosser than it really is.

BRING YOUR OWN Pencil sharpeners are used so often and by so many different people that they collect germs. They're considered the dirtiest thing in most classrooms.

RULES

ITCH-EROO Walking around barefoot in the gym locker room is a good way to pick up athlete's foot, a fungal infection that grows between the toes. Itching, burning, and redness are signs there's a problem.

BOOKWORM Seen in old books and books stored in dark, damp places, booklice congregate in large numbers. They thrive on the mold that grows between the pages and in the glue and binding materials. Despite their name, they're not actually lice.

SANDBOX SURPRISES A sandbox may look cleaner than dirt, but it's much grosser. Animals like raccoons and feral (wild) cats use them as litter boxes, leaving disgusting and dangerous waste behind.

IN THE LAB Experiments can be messy, stinky, and gross. That's what makes the science lab such a cool place to learn!

LOCATION MATTERS Germs from every cough, sneeze, and hand that touches it linger on a school desk. The desk nearest the door gets an extra dose when kids tap it on their way in or out of a classroom.

THAT'S OLD

CARNIVORE

HERBIVORE

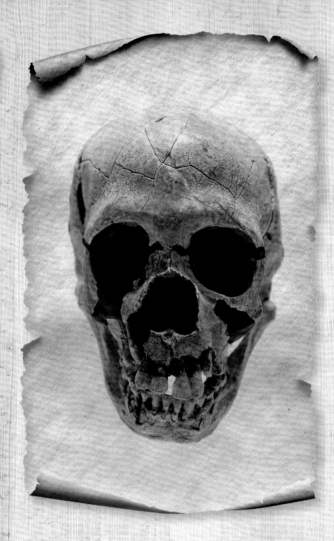

DROP IT LIKE A DINO Dinosaur droppings and fossilized poop from other animals are called coprolites. They don't smell, but they do tell. By studying coprolites, scientists can figure out whether a dinosaur was a carnivore (meat eater), herbivore (plant eater), or omnivore (ate both meat and plants). The shape of a coprolite lets experts know if it came from a dinosaur, fish, or other animal. The largest dinosaur coprolite discovered so far, found in Washington State in 2012, measured about 40 inches (about 1 meter) long.

TOOTH-TELLER Studying food on old teeth may sound gross, but scientists have discovered a lot about what Neanderthals ate by studying tooth fossils. There were no toothbrushes or dental floss, which means that 50,000-year-old teeth can tell tales about how Neanderthals lived and what they ate. Old food trapped in plaque shows that they ate meat and plants. In this case, poor dental hygiene was a good thing!

TEA TIME Goat poop and vinegar was mixed together as an energy drink in ancient Rome. Does that sound gross? In modern times, Moroccan argan tree-climbing goats poop out undigested seeds from the tree's fruits. People collect the seeds and turn them into oil for food and cosmetics.

GOOD GROOMING Vikings are often depicted as untidy, but there's evidence that they bathed weekly, made combs out of animal antlers, and used little spoons to clean out their ear wax. They were inventive too—they boiled a tree fungus in urine to create a kind of fire starter that they could carry with them.

SPACE GRUNGE

The International Space Station (ISS) is a satellite that orbits Earth. The astronauts on board work, exercise, relax, and sleep in a weightless environment. Here's the dirty truth on how they stay clean.

 **4** DAYS BETWEEN UNDERWEAR CHANGES According to NASA, the ISS crew would need 540 pairs of underwear for a typical six-month stay, and that would take up a lot of space and weigh things down. So astronauts stretch out how long they wear things.

 **1** WEEK WEARING THE SAME EXERCISE CLOTHES Astronauts need to exercise to avoid muscle and bone loss that can happen in a weightless environment. Blobs of sweat stick to the body and are collected to be recycled into drinking water.

 **3** MONTHS SOME ASTRONAUTS WEAR THE SAME PAIR OF SHORTS The air on the ISS is kept at an even temperature, so there isn't a lot of sweating during regular activities.

 **0** TIMES ASTRONAUTS DO LAUNDRY Unpiloted spacecraft make one-way trips to deliver supplies to the space station. Once the supplies have been unloaded, the spacecraft is packed with dirty laundry and trash, then set on a course to burn up in Earth's atmosphere over the Pacific Ocean.

 **80** PERCENT OF WATER IS RECYCLED With a limited amount of water on the space station, every possible drop—from sweat, the moisture in breath, and urine—is collected and purified for use in food preparation and for drinking.

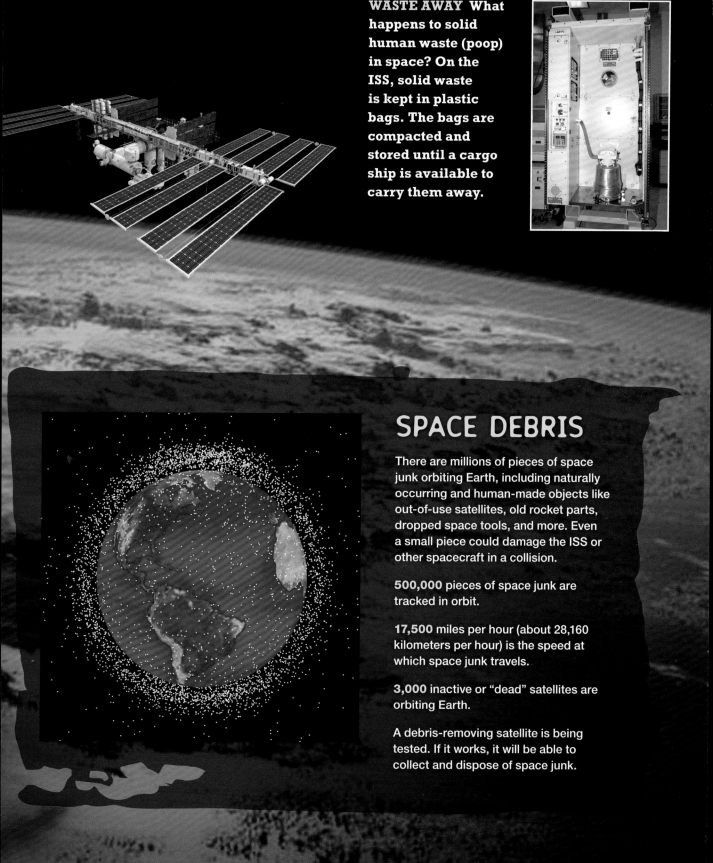

WASTE AWAY What happens to solid human waste (poop) in space? On the ISS, solid waste is kept in plastic bags. The bags are compacted and stored until a cargo ship is available to carry them away.

SPACE DEBRIS

There are millions of pieces of space junk orbiting Earth, including naturally occurring and human-made objects like out-of-use satellites, old rocket parts, dropped space tools, and more. Even a small piece could damage the ISS or other spacecraft in a collision.

500,000 pieces of space junk are tracked in orbit.

17,500 miles per hour (about 28,160 kilometers per hour) is the speed at which space junk travels.

3,000 inactive or "dead" satellites are orbiting Earth.

A debris-removing satellite is being tested. If it works, it will be able to collect and dispose of space junk.

BIG 10!

DIRTY WORK

Important jobs that keep things working!

SANITATION CREW

Rainy days are unpleasant for someone collecting garbage, but a hot, sunny day can raise the stink factor to unbearable.

SEWER WORKER

Sewer cleaners and inspectors are responsible for keeping water and waste from toilets, showers, and appliances moving through the sewer system. That includes removing yucky gunk that clogs things up.

DIAPER SERVICE WORKER

A baby can use 2,500 to 3,000 diapers in its first year. Some parents use cloth diapers, which are reusable, and send the dirty ones to a diaper service for cleaning.

EMBALMER

Embalmers preserve human bodies for funerals and burials, coming into contact with blood and other bodily fluids. They use sanitizers and other chemicals in their work.

COAL MINER

Working in a coal mine is hard, dangerous, and very dirty. Miners get dirty from the coal, and dust in the air can get into their lungs.

PORTABLE TOILET CLEANER

A vacuum-like machine and high-powered hose help workers remove the waste and clean portable toilets. When one turns over, it becomes a super messy job.

OIL RIG ROUGHNECK

Roughnecks do many jobs around an oil rig, including cleaning equipment. They get sprayed with oil and mud and covered with grease from the machinery.

BAT GUANO COLLECTOR

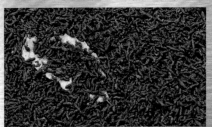

Bat guano (poop) is prized by organic gardeners as a natural fertilizer. Collecting it from caves can disturb bats, and conservationists are developing safe harvesting practices.

MANURE INSPECTOR

Before farm manure is used to create fertilizer, inspectors have the dirty job of digging through it looking for possible contaminants.

DAIRY FARMHAND

Dairy farmhands' tasks include feeding, operating milking equipment, and managing animal waste. A Holstein cow can produce more than 100 pounds (about 45 kilograms) of waste a day!

ATROCIOUS AQUATICS

Water, water, everywhere! It covers about 70 percent of Earth's surface and travels below, as well. That leads to lots of icky things.

GOO BALLS Harmless blobs called salps can be as small as your finger or as large as a shoebox. They're gooey, jelly-like animals, but they're plankton, not jellyfish. They stick together to form alarmingly long chains, sometimes reaching 50 feet (about 15 meters) in length.

HUGE HELPERS Blue whales are the largest animals on Earth. When they poop, they expel a long, orange plume that floats. Whales are like ocean gardeners, depositing fertilizer near the ocean's surface, where it provides nutrients for marine plants.

TRUE OR FALSE?

Fish don't pee.

False! The urine from saltwater fish is a food source for coral reefs. It's part of a healthy ocean ecosystem.

BIG BUT NOT GREAT The Great Pacific Garbage Patch includes more than 1.8 trillion pieces of plastic—the largest accumulation in the world. Eighty percent is land-based garbage, from drinking straws to industrial waste. It covers an area twice as big as the state of Texas. Scientists recommend limiting the use of disposable plastics as a way to help reduce the size and effects of this ocean dump.

Up, Up, and Away When a geyser erupts, water and steam shoot up from an underground hot spring. At Old Faithful in Yellowstone National Park, the water reaches an average height of 130 to 140 feet (about 40 to 43 meters). It is hot too—more than 200° Fahrenheit (about 93° Celsius). Hydrogen sulfide gas in the water makes it smell like rotten eggs.

COME ON IN! Pool filters and skimmers distribute bacteria-fighting chemicals and collect leaves, dirt, insects, and other gunk in the water. Cleaning out a skimmer basket can be a nasty task, though—sometimes there are drowned mice, snakes, and other small animals.

BIG 10! BEDROOM

MUCKY MATTRESSES Mattresses are dead skin collectors. Skin cells flake off while you sleep, and more than a pound (about .45 kilograms) of them sink into your mattress in a year.

SPRING SNEEZER
Pollen and dirt stick to curtain fabric. This can turn the bedroom into a sneeze zone during the spring, when airborne pollen is plentiful.

DREAMING AND DROOLING
People produce more than a quart (about a liter) of saliva each day. When we're awake, we swallow it. When we're asleep, the swallow reflex lessens and we drool onto our pillows.

TRY FOR DRY All it takes is one piece of damp clothing in the hamper to cause problems like mildew and give laundry a musty smell. That's bad for your clothes and your nose.

DOUBLE TROUBLE
Lampshades attract dust and insects. Static electricity makes the shade a magnet for dust, while moths are attracted to light and get zapped by hot bulbs.

BLUES

SCARY STORIES Silverfish are insects that eat starchy things like the paper and glue in books. They are nocturnal—they eat while you're asleep.

HIDDEN DIRT Carpets can look clean but be really gross. A square foot (about 929 square centimeters) of carpeting can trap up to a pound of dirt between its fibers.

WHAT SMELL? Your nose gets used to smells that you're around a lot. Called nose blindness, this is why you may not notice the stink of dirty laundry until someone comes in and says, "Ew, what's that smell?"

OLD AND COLD If you find an old slice of pizza under papers on your desk, don't eat it. Pizza can harbor food-borne bacteria if it sits at room temperature overnight.

THESE BUNNIES CAN'T HOP Dust bunnies hide under beds and other furniture. They look like large clumps of dust, but are often made up of hair, lint, dead skin, and mites.

LEARN MORE

MUSEUMS AND ZOOS

Natural History Museum of Los Angeles County
Los Angeles, CA
nhm.org

Visit the Insect Zoo at the Natural History Museum of Los Angeles County to see tarantulas, white-eyed assassin bugs, and more. They cosponsor an annual Bug Fair every spring, which includes live animal demonstrations and a bug chef cooking up tasty treats.

Museum of Life and Science
Durham, NC
lifeandscience.org

The Bayer Insectarium includes insects from around the world. But the ickiest and coolest thing to do may be walking through the open-air exhibit of giant orb weaver spiders.

The Mütter Museum of the College of Physicians of Philadelphia
Philadelphia, PA
muttermuseum.org

This medical museum includes a collection of 139 human skulls, specimens of Einstein's brain, and a wide variety of medical instruments.

Disgusting Food Museum
Malmö, Sweden
disgustingfoodmuseum.com

Foods that people in one place think are delicious may sound gross to others. This museum explores foods with a reputation for being disgusting. Visitors can smell and taste some of the foods. A traveling exhibit landed in Los Angeles recently. One can only hope for more special exhibits in the future.

WEBSITES

Learn more about the Great Pacific Garbage Patch and how to get involved in cleaning up the beaches and ocean.

theoceancleanup.com/great-pacific-garbage patch/

Read about living on the International Space Station.

nasa.gov/audience/foreducators/stem-on-station/dayinthelife

PHOTO CREDITS